These pages may be copied.

Permission is granted to the buyer of this book to reproduce, duplicate or photocopy these materials for use with students in Sunday school or Bible teaching classes.

Rainbow Publishers • P.O. Box 261129 • San Diego, CA 92196

HANDS-ON NATURE FOR GRADES 1&2
©1999 by Rainbow Publishers
ISBN 1-885358-66-0
Rainbow reorder# RB36863

Rainbow Publishers
P.O. Box 261129
San Diego, CA 92196

Cover and interior art: Chuck Galey
Editor: Christy Allen

Scriptures are from the *Holy Bible: New International Version* (North American Edition), copyright ©1973, 1978, 1984 by the International Bible Society. Used by permission of Zondervan Bible Publishers.

All rights reserved.

Printed in the United States of America

Contents

Memory Verse Index 6

Introduction 7

All About Nature 9
God Is Faithful in Creation 11
Keep a Nature Notebook 13
Nature Mobiles 15
Pocket Microscope 18
This Is My Father's World 19
Touch-N-Feel Books 22
Worship Outdoors 25

God's Green Earth 27
Amazing Nature 28
Autumn Leaf Messages 29
Bark Rubbings 32
Flower Decoupage 33
God's Gold Mine 34
Leaf Creatures 36
Mother Nature Preserves 37
Pine Cone Flowers 38
Rock Game 40
Sand Casting 42
Seed Pencil Holder 43
The Happy Man Is Like a Tree 45
Twig Weaving 47
Twig Wreath 48
Types of Soil 49

Animal Adventures 51
A Little Birdie Told Them 52
Birds in the Bible Crossword 53
Blowfish 55
Hiding Places 57
Nature's Intricacies 58
Worm Houses 60

Outdoor Observations 61
Crazy Clouds 62
God Is Faithful Nature Pantomime 63
Make a Rainbow 63
God's Control of Seasons 64
God's Gift of Weather 69
Making Rain 72
Raindrop Preservation 73
Shadow Clock 74
Star Gaze 75
Star-Studded Peep Boxes 76
Static Electricity 77
The Seasons Table Scene 78
Wind Speed 80

Food Fun 83
Fruits of the Spirit 85
God Gives Us Variety 87
Growing Vines 89
How Does Your Garden Grow? 91
Let's Paint Apples 92
Pomanders 93
Pumpkins and Leaves 95
Seeking Light 96

Memory Verse Index

Old Testament

Genesis 1:20	Blowfish	55
Genesis 1:29-30	Touch-N-Feel Books	22
Genesis 8:22	The Seasons Table Scene	78
Genesis 9:13	Make a Rainbow	63
Leviticus 26:3-4	Raindrop Preservation	73
1 Kings 17:4-6	A Little Birdie Told Them	52
2 Kings 19:15	Mother Nature Preserves	37
Job 37:11-12	God's Control of Seasons	64
Psalm 1:3	The Happy Man Is Like a Tree	45
Psalm 1:3	Pumpkins and Leaves	95
Psalm 8:3	Star Gaze	75
Psalm 8:6	Sand Casting	42
Psalm 17:8-9	Hiding Places	57
Psalm 34:1	God Gives Us Variety	87
Psalm 40:2	Rock Game	40
Psalm 45:7	Pomanders	93
Psalm 75:1	Worship Outdoors	25
Psalm 89:1	God Is Faithful Nature Pantomime	63
Psalm 97:6	Crazy Clouds	62
Psalm 104:14	How Does Your Garden Grow?	91
Psalm 104:24	God's Gold Mine	34
Psalm 104:24	Keep a Nature Notebook	13
Psalm 104:24	Nature Mobiles	15
Psalm 105:1-2	Autumn Leaf Messages	29
Psalm 136:1, 7-8	Let's Paint Apples	92
Psalm 136:1, 7-9	Shadow Clock	74
Psalm 145:5	Pocket Microscope	18
Psalm 146:5-6	Birds in the Bible Crossword	53
Psalm 147:4-5	Star-Studded Peep Boxes	76
Psalm 148:7-8	Static Electricity	77
Ecclesiastes 3:11	Nature's Intricacies	58
Isaiah 35:1	Flower Decoupage	33
Isaiah 40:22	Twig Wreath	48
Isaiah 41:19	Pine Cone Flowers	38
Isaiah 41:19-20	Bark Rubbings	32
Jeremiah 10:13	God's Gift of Weather	69
Jeremiah 32:17	Fruits of the Spirit	85
Lam. 3:22-23	God Is Faithful in Creation	11
Ezekiel 47:12	Leaf Creatures	36
Joel 2:23	Making Rain	72

New Testament

Matthew 6:26	Worm Houses	60
Matthew 7:24, 26	Types of Soil	49
Matthew 17:20	Seed Pencil Holder	43
Mark 4:41	Wind Speed	80
Luke 9:43	Amazing Nature	28
Luke 12:27	This Is My Father's World	19
John 12:46	Seeking Light	96
John 15:1-2	Growing Vines	89
Romans 11:16	Twig Weaving	47

Introduction

This book is written to help children experience and connect spiritual truths to the wonder of God's creation in interactive — Hands-On! — ways. You will find that the lessons encourage your students to make full use of their senses. And you will appreciate the ease in planning the lessons. By gathering basic supplies like paper towel rolls and toothpicks, you can teach several different nature lessons.

All of the games, crafts and activities in *Hands-On Nature* were created especially for the interests and abilities of first- and second-graders. Each activity may be used as a self-contained lesson or as an addition to your curriculum. There is no specific order to the lessons — simply select a topic you want to teach and let the book guide you through the lesson. To maximize the learning opportunity for your students, there is an objective, memory verse and prayer with every lesson.

God created a beautiful world for us to enjoy. Help children understand God's "hands-on" role in their lives and their world.

All About Nature

    God Is Faithful in Creation 11

    Keep a Nature Notebook 13

    Nature Mobiles 15

    Pocket Microscope 18

    This Is My Father's World 19

    Touch-N-Feel Books 22

    Worship Outdoors 25

The heavens declare the glory of God;
the skies proclaim the work of his hands. Psalm 19:1

God Is Faithful in Creation

 ## Objective
To help children realize God's faithfulness

 ## Memory Verse
Because of the Lord's great love we are not consumed, for his compassions never fail. They are new every morning; great is your faithfulness. **Lamentations 3:22-23**

 ## Prayer
Thank You, dear God, for showing us Your faithfulness through the things You have created, how You make everything to work together for our good. We love You. Amen.

Teach
Take the children on a walk around outside of the building. Tell them to look for things in nature that God has made to show His faithfulness.

What to Do
1. Give each child a copy of page 12 and have the students write short poems or sentences about what they saw.
2. Encourage them to think colorfully and creatively.
3. Let them share their poems and thoughts. Examples:
   "God's white clouds gather high in the sky. He pours out His rain, so the earth won't be dry." "We saw the autumn trees and the autumn leaves. The leaves were brown and green when we saw them. But God can make them any color He wants. I love God."

God is Faithful

Because of the Lord's great love we are not consumed, for his compassions never fail. They are new every morning; great is your faithfulness.

Lamentations 3:22-23

Keep a Nature Notebook

 Objective
To encourage children to make the study of nature a lifelong adventure

 Memory Verse
How many are your works, O Lord! In wisdom you made them all; the earth is full of your creatures. **Psalm 104:24**

 Prayer
Father in heaven, how thankful we are that You loved us enough to create so many wonderful things for us to enjoy and learn about. Amen.

Teach

Duplicate the Nature Notebooks for each child from page 14. Give each child several copies. If desired, have them attach construction paper covers for them. Following are some suggestions for how to explain the project:

- Date

    This will tell when the nature study was conducted. It can provide valuable information about findings during a particular time of the year.

- Time

    The time of day or night can be significant. Many things in nature change depending on whether they are observed in the daytime or at night.

- Weather

    Record the temperature, cloud formations, rain, snow, wind conditions and other weather information. By maintaining good records, nature can be predicted by how it is affected by weather.

- Location

    Be specific about the location: "on the right side of the front porch next to the knothole." Then if it is necessary to find the location again, they can go directly to it.

- Illustrations

    Drawings are an important part of recording information. These do not need to be artistic, just able to be interpreted. A photograph can also be included.

- Types of Study

    Students might want to separate their notebooks into sections, or perhaps even have separate notebooks for the different types of nature.

Illustrations

Date: _____

Time: _____

Weather: _____

Location: _____

Nature Mobiles

 ## Objective
To teach children about all the different things in nature

 ## Memory Verse
How many are your works, O Lord! In wisdom you made them all; the earth is full of your creatures. **Psalm 104:24**

 ## Prayer
Dear God, when we look around us we see so many different things You created for us to enjoy. Thank You for giving us so much. We love You. Amen.

Teach
Discuss God's greatness in being able to make so many different kinds of things in nature for people to enjoy. Ask the children to name their favorites.

You Will Need
- pages 16 and 17
- poster board
- construction paper
- scissors
- hangers
- string
- tape

Before Class
Cut out the patterns from page 16 and 17 and trace onto poster board. Cut out the poster board templates. Depending on the size of the class, you may want to make several of each template.

What to Do
1. Have the children select shapes they like and trace them onto construction paper.
2. Instruct the students to cut out the shapes.
3. Allow the children to cut varying lengths of string for their mobiles.
4. Show how to tape the string to the shapes and to the coat hanger.

Pocket Microscope

 Objective
To show nature's wonders to the smallest degree

 Memory Verse
I will meditate on your wonderful works.
Psalm 145:5

 Prayer
Thank You, O God, for the mysteries of your creation, and thank You for providing a way for us to see some of them. You are so very good to us. We love You. Amen.

Teach
Say, **Many things in nature are too small to see with the naked eye. We need help to see the wonders of the things of nature that God has created. God gave mankind knowledge to know how to make tools to use to see these things.** The children can make their own microscopes to use in viewing some of these mysteries and wonders.

You Will Need
- paper towel rolls
- crayons
- plastic wrap
- rubber bands
- pencils
- water
- salt or sugar
- seeds

Before Class
Cut the paper towel rolls in half, one half per child. Write the memory verse on each one. Gather together several tiny items for observation, such as salt or sugar and seeds.

What to Do
1. Give each child a paper towel roll half. Allow the students to color the tube.
2. Explain how to fit a piece of plastic wrap firmly over one end of the tube and secure it in place with a rubber band.
3. Show how to hold the tube vertical, with the plastic-wrapped end down. To make space for a drop of water in the middle of the plastic, give each child a pencil and have them press the eraser end down into the opening end of the tube and press it against the center of the plastic to form a slight cup.
4. Help each child put a couple of drops of water into the cup made by the eraser.
5. Demonstrate how to hold the wrapped end (the lens end) close to the object to be magnified and how to hold your eye to the open end of the tube. As you look through the drops of water, things will be magnified.
6. Ask, **What does a grain of salt or sugar look like? How many legs does a tiny insect have? Are tiny seeds smooth or bumpy?**

This Is My Father's World

Objective
To increase children's appreciation for God's love and nearness as expressed through the beauties of nature

Memory Verse
Consider how the lilies grow. They do not labor or spin. Yet I tell you, not even Solomon in all his splendor was dressed like one of these. **Luke 12:27**

Prayer
Dear God, thank You for creating our world and all the things it holds. Thank You for eyes to see and ears to hear. We love You. Amen.

Teach

Sing or read together the hymn "This Is My Father's World" (see lyrics below). Cut out and color the pictures on pages 20 and 21 that depict the things in the hymn and hold them up at the appropriate phrase. Discuss with the children what the hymn teaches about God's wonders in nature.

This Is My Father's World

This is my Father's world,
And to my list'ning ears
All nature sings, and round me rings
The music of the spheres.
This is my Father's world.
I rest me in the thought
Of rocks and trees, of skies and seas —
His hand the wonders wrought.
(Babcock, 1901/traditional English melody; adapt. by Franklin L. Sheppard, 1915)

1. "My Father's World" (globe)
   Discussion: Why do we call this God's world? Where, in the Bible, do we find the story of Creation?
2. "My list'ning ears" (child outdoors listening)
   Discussion: What do you know about your ears? About sound waves? Do you know some animals can hear sounds we cannot? Why might God create them so?
3. "All nature sings, and round me rings the music of the spheres" (bird)
   Discussion: Tell some sounds of God's world that you have heard. By what inventions has man put God's laws of sound to work? (radio, telephone, record player, etc.)
4. "Rocks and Trees" (rocks and trees)
   Discussion: Have any of you made a collection of rocks? Could you bring them to show us next Sunday? How are trees useful to us? (food, lumber, paper, shade) How can we protect our nation's trees?
5. "Skies and seas" (ocean scene)
   Discussion: When you think of the skies, what is the first thing that comes to your mind? What do you think of when you hear the word "seas"?
6. "His hand the wonders wrought" (nature scene)
   Discussion: What does this phrase mean? Who will look up the word "wrought" in the dictionary?

Sing verse one together again, then have the children offer prayers thanking God for our wonderful world.

Touch-N-Feel Books

 Objective
To teach awareness of the many kinds of things that are in nature and awareness of the greatness of God's work in nature

 Memory Verse
Then God said, "I give you every seed-bearing plant on the face of the whole earth and every tree that has fruit with seed in it. They will be yours for food. And to all the beasts of the earth and all the birds of the air and all the creatures that move on the ground...I give every green plant for food." **Genesis 1:29-30**

 Prayer
Dear God, our world is so full of so many wonderful things You created — the birds, the animals and the plants. Thank You for giving them to us. Amen.

Teach
Have the children express their feelings about the trees, flowers, animals, etc., that are found in nature and how good God is in giving such things. Say, **Touch-n-feel books are fun, and they teach a lot about all the kinds of things that God gave us in the nature around us. Let's make one.**

You Will Need
- pages 23 and 24
- stapler
- tape
- cotton
- dried peas
- feathers
- blue plastic wrap
- tree bark
- leaves
- glue
- crayons

Before Class
Duplicate pages 23 and 24 for each child.

What to Do
1. Give each child a copy of pages 23-24.
2. Show how to fold the paper into book form. Staple each book at the binding and place tape over the staples to avoid injury.
3. Give the children the appropriate items to glue on the pages: cotton on sheep, peas on turtle, feathers on bird, plastic wrap on waterfall and bark and leaves on tree.
4. Allow the students to color the pictures.

24

Worship Outdoors

 Objective

To increase an awareness of God's nearness outdoors; to encourage children to draw close and talk to Him while enjoying the beauties of nature

 Memory Verse

We give thanks to you, O God, we give thanks, for your Name is near; men tell of your wonderful deeds. **Psalm 75:1**

 Prayer

Dear God, thank You for giving us such a beautiful world. Thank You for being ever-present and near no matter where we are. We love You. Amen.

Teach

Read the brief sketches below of Bible people who worshipped God outdoors and have the children guess who the Bible characters are. Note: Try not to let a child who knows the Bible well monopolize all of the answers. Use him or her to read some of the sketches or look up the Bible references and read them after the others have given answers.

1. I lived long before there were churches. I would sit outside my tent home and study the stars. I knew there must be a great God who made all things. I tried to worship Him. Then in a very real way He talked to me and told me I must take my family and go on a long journey which He would show me. The journey took us many weeks, but I found that God was with us and we had nothing to fear if we drew near to Him, listened to His instructions and obeyed His leading. (Answer: Abraham; Genesis 12:1)

2. I stole from my brother and lied to my dad. I got into such trouble I had to leave home. We did not have cars like you have today. I had to walk. My heart was troubled because of all the wrong things I had done. I wondered if God cared about me and could forgive and help me. One lonely night I slept out under the stars on a big rock, but I found I was not alone. God's spirit came close to me. He showed me a vision of angels and said, "I am the Lord God of your father. I am with you and will keep you wherever you go." When I awoke I set up a stone for an altar and promised God that I would live for Him. (Answer: Jacob; Genesis 28:16)

3. I cared for my father's sheep and found I could draw near to God right out in the fields. I played on my flute and harp and made up songs of praise to God. When I faced dangerous wild animals, like a bear and a lion, God was near to help. When the danger was past, I would praise and thank God. He was near and like a shepherd to me. (Answer: David; 1 Samuel 17:37)

4. I liked to go away by myself into the mountains. There, no one would bother me, and I could feel close to my heavenly Father. Sometimes I spent all night alone in prayer. The night when the soldiers came to take me, I was outdoors in a garden talking to my heavenly Father. His nearness gave me strength to face suffering and death. (Answer: Jesus; Luke 6:12)

5. God directed me to go to a lonely desert road, where few people traveled. As I waited to learn what God wanted of me there, a chariot with an Ethiopian man came near. He was reading from the prophecy of Isaiah, a Scripture about the promised Messiah. He stopped his chariot and I had a chance to tell him about Jesus. The Lord's presence seemed near to us. The Ethiopian man believed in Jesus and was baptized. We worshipped God outdoors that day. (Answer: Philip; Acts 8:30)

6. I was a businesswoman, a saleslady who sold beautiful cloth to rich people. One day the missionary Paul came to our city. On the Sabbath day he met with a group of us outdoors by a riverside. There he preached to us about Jesus and we prayed together. I accepted Jesus as my Savior and was baptized. I worshipped God outdoors. (Answer: Lydia; Acts 16:14)

God's Green Earth

Amazing Nature 28
Autumn Leaf Messages 29
Bark Rubbings 32
Flower Decoupage 33
God's Gold Mine 34
Leaf Creatures 36
Mother Nature Preserves 37
Pine Cone Flowers 38
Rock Game 40
Sand Casting 42
Seed Pencil Holder 43
The Happy Man Is Like a Tree 45
Twig Weaving 47
Twig Wreath 48
Types of Soil 49

The wilderness will rejoice and blossom. Isaiah 35:1

Amazing Nature

 **Objective**
To encourage children to be in awe at the greatness and power of God in, through and with His creations

 Memory Verse
And they were all amazed at the greatness of God. **Luke 9:43**

 Prayer
Dear God, there is no end to Your wonderful creations. You are indeed a Great God who is worthy of our praise and love. Amen.

Teach
Say, **God is not only the Creator, He is a Healer, Provider and Protector. Sometimes He uses surprising ways to accomplish what He wants. He often surprises us with His power. Can you think of some of God's creations that have surprised you? Here's one that you may not have found before.** Do the dandelion experiment below with the class.

You Will Need
- dandelions

What to Do
1. Say, **God put elastic material in dandelions!**
2. Give each child a dandelion. Show how to break the stem.
3. Show how to squeeze the sap from the stem and use it to coat the end of your finger up to your first knuckle.
4. Let the sap dry for a few minutes.
5. Have the students gently roll the dry, rubbery sap off their fingers, like rolling a sock off of a foot.
6. Pull the sap in different directions. Ask, **What happens to the sap?**
7. Say, **Sap is a juice that flows through plants, carrying food and water to all plant parts. The dandelion sap dries to form an elastic material. When it dries, it becomes stretchable, like a rubber band. What a surprise in God's creation! Isn't He great?**

Autumn Leaf Messages

 Objective
To help children see beauty and God's goodness in everything around us and to share it with others

 Memory Verse
Give thanks to the Lord, call on his name; make known among the nations what he has done. Sing to him, sing praise to him; tell of all his wonderful acts. **Psalm 105:1-2**

 Prayer
Thank You, dear God, for the beautiful things in nature that You give us to enjoy and share. Amen.

Teach
Explain how God created nature for us to enjoy. Then discuss with the children how it feels to give a present to someone. Ask, **How can we share God's gift of nature as a gift to someone else?**

You Will Need
- pages 30 and 31
- construction paper in fall colors
- scissors
- glue
- pencils
- dark-colored tissue
- ribbon

Before Class
Make several copies of pages 30 and 31 and cut out the leaves to use as templates.

What to Do
1. Place the leaf templates around the classroom table.
2. Allow each child to trace leaf shapes on construction paper and cut them out.
3. Have them write or glue on each leaf a Scripture verse, small cartoon, joke or poem.
4. Show how to glue the finished leaves like fallen autumn leaves on a sheet of tissue.
5. Demonstrate how to roll the tissue into a scroll and tie with a ribbon.
6. Send the scrolls to shut-ins, classmates who are ill, nursing home residents or a children's hospital.

Bark Rubbings

 Objective

To help children not only to know that God created the world and all that is within it, but that He created many different kinds of trees, flowers and plants, animals, and people who are to live together in harmony

 Memory Verse

I will set pines in the wasteland, the fir and the cypress together, so that people may see and know…that the hand of the Lord…has created it. **Isaiah 41:19-20**

 Prayer

Dear God, You are a great and wonderful God. You have made everything different, yet You have given us the love of Jesus to help us all live together. Thank You. Amen.

Teach
Say, **What part of a tree do you see most clearly? You see the trunk and the bark covering it. Tree bark comes in a lot of colors and textures. Paper birch trees have light-colored bark that peels off. North American Indian tribes used it to make canoes. Maple trees have gray, shaggy bark. Beech trees have smooth bark. Sometimes the bark on a tree's branches looks different from the bark on its trunk. That's because the trunk is the oldest part of the tree, so its bark tends to be thicker, darker, or more deeply furrowed. You can identify some trees just by the color of their bark. For instance, you can recognize a sycamore tree by its patches that look like a quilt. Sweet cherry trees have deep red bark with thin black stripes circling the trunk. A tree's bark is its protective outer "skin." Just beneath is the inner bark, which carries sap to feed the tree and supply energy to its roots. The bark of some trees, such as birches, really is as thin as skin. Redwood trees, though, have bark as much as a foot thick, and the bark of a giant sequoia tree can be two feet thick!** Have a reference book on trees available for the class to see pictures of the trees as you describe them. Then take a walk outdoors, make some bark rubbings (see directions below), and use the reference book to try to identify the different trees.

You Will Need
• construction paper   • crayons   • tape

Before Class
Remove the paper wrappers from the crayons.

What to Do
1. Allow each child to select several sheets of construction paper and crayons.
2. Instruct the students to find an interesting patch of bark and tape a piece of construction paper over it.
3. Show how to hold a crayon against the tree and rub up and down over the paper, pressing firmly. Have the students continue coloring until they get an interesting pattern on their sheets.
4. Have the children remove the tape and inspect their bark rubbings. Encourage them to try different trees and look at the different patterns they get.
5. After the class returns to the classroom, allow the students to write the name of the tree and the memory verse on each of their rubbings.

Flower Decoupage

 Objective
To help children see and feel the joy of God's creation and all that He has to offer

 Memory Verse
The wilderness will rejoice and blossom.
Isaiah 35:1

 Prayer
Dear God, help us to sing out with joy and praise because of all You have given us and all You do for us. We love You. Amen.

Teach

Decoupage is a way of decorating an object with pictures, cutouts, or, in this case, flowers and leaves. The decoration is protected and made to look beautiful by coatings of a clear, hard finish.

You Will Need

- dried flowers and leaves
- paper plates
- crayons
- glue
- tweezers
- paint brushes
- plastic wrap
- hole punch
- yarn

What to Do

1. Give each child a paper plate.
2. Allow the children to decorate the inside rim of the paper plate with a crayon design. Encourage them to copy the memory verse on the rim.
3. Pour liquid white glue into paper cups and make them accessible.
4. Show how to paint the bottom of the inside of the plate with a coating of the glue.
5. Instruct the students to carefully pick up the dried flowers and leaves and arrange them in a pattern on the plate. Tweezers can be used to help pick up and place the objects.
6. Have the children lightly paint a second coat of glue over the flowers. Allow the glue to dry completely. While the plate is drying, cover the glue in the cup with plastic wrap or foil to keep it from drying out.
7. Allow the students to give the entire plate a second coating of glue after the first coating has dried.
8. When the hangings are dry, show how to punch a hole in the top of the plate and thread a piece of yarn through. Make a knot in the yarn and use for a hanger.

God's Gold Mine

 Objective
To bring awareness of the fullness of God's creation

 Memory Verse
How many are your works, O Lord! **Psalm 104:24**

 Prayer
Thank You, dear God, for Your rich gifts to us so we can share the beauty of all You have made. Amen.

Teach
Read Psalm 104:24. Say, **This verse says the earth is full of God's riches — like a gold mine! What are some of the things you like best about God's earth? Which creation do you think God values most?** (people)

You Will Need
- page 35
- nature items (see below)
- construction paper
- glue

Before Class
Duplicate page 35 on construction paper for each child.

What to Do
1. Take the children on a field trip to gather items. Or have a good supply of leaves, weeds, rocks, flowers, moss, small twigs, etc., on hand.
2. Spread out and explore these various items from God's creation. Say, **How unique they are, how different…just like people!**
3. Give each child a copy of page 35. Have them glue the items on the paper, making a creative picture.
4. As the class works, talk about the many riches God has given. Have the children share and explain their pictures with one another.
5. Close with a circle prayer. Ask each person to thank God that the earth is full of His riches.

God's Gold Mine

How many are your works, O Lord!
Psalm 104:24

Leaf Creatures

 Objective
To teach children that we can have the living water that Jesus provides so that we will grow to be strong and fruitful Christians

 Memory Verse
Fruit trees of all kinds will grow on both banks of the river. Their leaves will not wither, nor will their fruit fail. Every month they will bear, because the water from the sanctuary flows to them. **Ezekiel 47:12**

 Prayer
Dear God, thank You for giving us the nourishment we need to grow and change into Christ-like men and women who will live for You. Amen.

Teach
Help the children collect many different kinds of fallen leaves of different colors. Discuss how God created so many different kinds of trees, just like so many different kinds of people, and how He nourishes them as they go through the natural changes. Say, **Jesus gives us that same nourishment as we make changes in our lives to live like Him.**

You Will Need
- construction paper
- glue
- small buttons, seeds or other decorations
- newspaper

What to Do
1. Have children find a nice large leaf for the body and a smaller one for the head. Skinny leaves are good to use for arms and legs. Small pointed leaves make fingers or ears.
2. Provide construction paper, glue and small buttons, seeds or other decorations to make eyes, noses, mouths, etc., on the leaf creatures.
3. When the leaf creatures are finished, press them for several weeks between a few sheets of newspaper. Put some heavy books on top of the newspaper to keep them flat so the leaves will not curl.

Mother Nature Preserves

 ## Objective
To encourage appreciation for God's creation

 ## Memory Verse
O Lord, God of Israel, enthroned between the cherubim, you alone are God over all the kingdoms of the earth. You have made heaven and earth. **2 Kings 19:15**

 ## Prayer
Dear God, we cannot even begin to count all of the kinds of things You have created. Thank You for giving us so much. We love You. Amen.

Teach
Have the children express their feelings about God and how He created all of the things below for their pleasure. Ask them to explain why they chose the nature items they selected.

You Will Need
- clear glass jars with lids
- modeling clay
- permanent marker

Before Class
Take the children on a field trip to gather seeds, weeds, flowers, leaves, twigs, bark, etc., or bring a large supply to use in this project. Write the memory verse on each jar with a permanent marker.

What to Do
1. Give each child a jar and some modeling clay.
2. Show how to put some modeling clay on the inside of the jar lid. Be sure not to spread the clay too close to the edge of the lid. There must be room to put it back on the jar later.
3. Explain how to arrange the plants and other items in the clay to create a nature scene. Miniature ceramic or plastic animals can be added to the scene.
4. Help the children place the jars carefully over the arrangements and tighten the lids. This arrangement will last a long time if kept airtight.

Pine Cone Flowers

 Objective
To provide a remembrance to children of this Scripture where God declares that He is the Great Creator

 Memory Verse
I will set pines in the wasteland. **Isaiah 41:19**

 Prayer
Dear God, You are so wise and so powerful, yet You love even the tiniest part of Your creation. Thank You for loving me. Amen.

Teach
Say, **A pine cone looks very much like a flower made of wood. Just like a flower, a pine cone has petals that are closed while it is growing. When the cones are fully grown, they open their petals and spread their seeds so that new trees can grow.** Make a bouquet of cone flowers to decorate the classroom or for each child to take home. The flowers can be given to others as gifts, and the children can use the occasion to tell about God, who created everything!

You Will Need
- pattern from page 39
- construction paper
- pine cones
- chenille wire
- scissors
- plastic drinking straws
- glue

Before Class
Each child will need several cones, which can be of various sizes. Duplicate the pattern on page 39 onto several colors of construction paper.

What to Do
1. Show how to wrap a piece of chenille wire around the last ring of petals at the bottom of a pine cone.
2. Have the students twist the ends together, leaving one end of the wire longer than the other end.
3. Allow the children to select a color of memory verse petal, cut it out and push the longer end of the wire through the center of the paper petal.
4. Give each child a plastic drinking straw and show how to twist the end of the wire tightly around it to make stems for the flowers. You may need to add a dab of glue to hold the wire in place.
5. Allow to dry overnight.

Rock Game

Objective
To help children remember that trust in God will give a solid place to stand so that they will not sink in sin

Memory Verse
He set my feet on a rock and gave me a firm place to stand. **Psalm 40:2**

Prayer
Dear God, how blessed we are that You not only created things for us to use for food, clothing and to build our homes, but You created things for us to use for play. Help us to remember that You are the solid rock in our lives and help us to stand on Your promises. Amen.

Teach
Discuss the difference between having a solid foundation to stand on and standing on mud. Ask, **Which is the better way to live?** To help remember this Scripture lesson, have the children make the game below using rocks.

You Will Need
- page 41
- small stones
- permanent markers
- crayons
- coffee cans
- construction paper
- tape

Before Class
Wash and dry 15 to 20 small, smooth stones per child. Duplicate page 41 for each child.

What to Do
1. Say, **The Indians used natural things in their games. They played many games that involved rolling stones. This was one game that they could play inside their teepee when the weather was too bad to play outdoors.** Each child can make a game to take home, or make one to use in the classroom.
2. Show the students how to use a permanent marker to write an X on five stones, an O on five stones, a Z on five stones and an E on five stones.
3. Give each child a copy of page 41 and allow the students to color the page.
4. Give each child a large, clean coffee can.
5. Show how to wrap the sheet around the coffee can and tape it on. Instruct the students to fill in where the sheet does not cover the can with construction paper.
6. To play the game, each player in turn puts his or her hand in the can (no peeking) and takes out one stone. Continue until all of the stones are picked from the can. The player who has the most of one letter wins the round. Repeat the game several times.

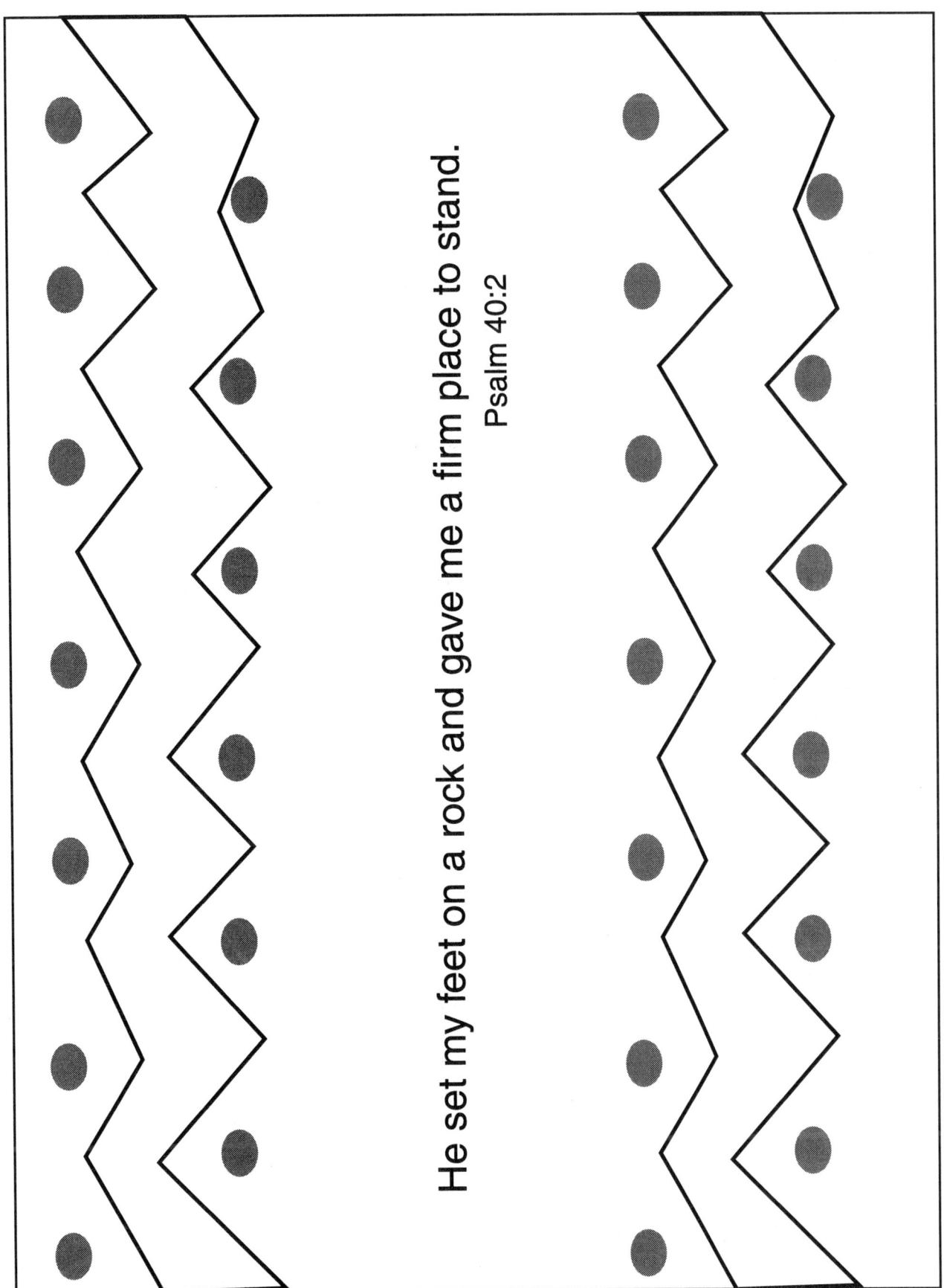

He set my feet on a rock and gave me a firm place to stand.
Psalm 40:2

Sand Casting

 Objective
To show children how nature can be used to make other things

 Memory Verse
You made him ruler over the works of your hands, you put everything under his feet. **Psalm 8:6**

 Prayer
Dear God, thank You for Your great plan of Creation and for giving us the knowledge to be able to use so many of the things to make other things to enjoy and use. Amen.

Teach
Discuss how wonderful it is to be able to use different things in nature to make other things, like sand and water to make a picture, trees to make houses, cotton to make clothing, etc. Ask, **How many other things can you name?**

You Will Need
- shoe boxes
- sand
- water
- paper clips
- stones
- plaster of Paris

Before Class
You will need one shoe box for each child.

What to Do
1. Fill each shoe box with moist sand.
2. Encourage the children to make shapes of flowers, animals and other nature items in the sand by making indents with their hands or a stick.
3. Small objects may be placed upside down in the sand.
4. When the students are ready, pour one inch of plaster of Paris over the entire sand surface. Before it sets, insert a paper clip at the top for a hanger.
5. After the plaster has hardened, gently lift the casting out of the box and brush off the excess sand.

Seed Pencil Holder

 Objective
To encourage children to increase their faith in God by trusting Him for all their needs

 Memory Verse
If you have faith as small as a mustard seed…nothing will be impossible for you.
Matthew 17:20

 Prayer
Dear God, thank You for loving me and for Your promise to keep me in Your care. Help me to have faith and trust in You. Amen.

Teach
Say, **We will remember this Scripture every time we see a seed. So, let's keep lots of seeds before us so we will always remember to put our entire trust and faith in God.**

You Will Need
- page 44
- clean 14-16 oz. cans
- paper cups
- glue
- paint brushes
- seeds
- tape

Before Class
Duplicate page 44 for each child.

What to Do
1. Give each child a copy of page 44.
2. Have the students lay the paper on a sheet of newspaper.
3. Pour glue into paper cups.
4. Show how to paint a section of the sheet with the glue, a little way in from the end. Sprinkle one kind of seed to the glued area. Blow away any seeds that have not fallen onto the glue.
5. Then have the children paint another area with glue and sprinkle on another kind of seed. Again, blow away any extra seeds.
6. Instruct the students to cover the paper with seeded areas — but warn them not to cover up the memory verse or the very ends of the paper (they will be taped together when the paper is placed on the can).
7. Allow the paper to dry overnight.
8. Show how to carefully roll the seeded paper around the can and overlap the ends that have no seeds glued to them.
9. The ends should be taped together. Allow the children to paint glue over this area and sprinkle seeds on it.
10. When everything is completely dry, paint over the entire surface with glue. Say, **Put pencils and pens in the can and place it where you will remember every day to have faith in God.**

If you have
faith as small as
a mustard seed...
nothing will be
impossible for you.
Matthew 17:20

The Happy Man Is Like a Tree

Objective
To think of the beauty and usefulness of a good tree and to compare it to the happy Christian

Memory Verse
He is like a tree planted by streams of water, which yields its fruit in season and whose leaf does not wither. Whatever he does prospers.
Psalm 1:3

Prayer
Dear God, You placed so many different kinds of trees in our world for our use, enjoyment and example. Help us to grow strong and straight like a good tree so that our lives will be useful, enjoyable and a good example to others. Thank You. Amen.

Teach
Discuss trees — their purpose (shade, fruit, nuts, building materials, etc.), and their characteristics (spindly, strong, evergreen, flowering, etc.). Ask, **How do these compare to people? What types of trees** (or what characteristics) **describe a Christian? Use the activity on page 46 to help you teach more about trees.**

Divide the class into two teams and see which one can find the most correct answers to the following tree quiz in a given amount of time.

1. What tree is spoken of as the king of trees? (Judges 9:8-15)
Answer: thornbush
2. To what tree does the Psalmist compare a wicked person? (Psalm 37:35)
Answer: green tree
3. On what kind of trees did the Israelites hang their harps while in Babylon? (Psalm 137:1-2)
Answer: poplars
4. Nathanael was under what tree when Jesus first called him? (John 1:48)
Answer: fig

5. David was to attack the Philistines on one occasion when he heard a "sound of marching" in the tops of what trees? (2 Samuel 5:24)
Answer: balsam
6. Zacchaeus climbed into what tree to view Jesus passing by? (Luke 19:4)
Answer: sycamore fig tree
7. From what kind of tree did Aaron's rod come? (Numbers 17:8)
Answer: almond
8. A lover was compared to what kind of tree by Solomon in his writings? (Song of Solomon 2:3)
Answer: apple

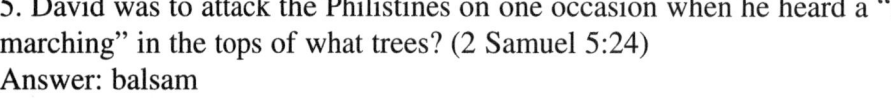

9. Absalom lost his life when his head was caught in what tree? (2 Samuel 18:9)
Answer: oak
10. After fleeing from the wicked Queen Jezebel, under what tree did Elijah rest? (1 Kings 19:4)
Answer: broom tree
11. The carpenter plants and the rain sustains what tree? (Isaiah 44:13-14)
Answer: pine
12. Ship boards were made from what tree? (Ezekiel 27:5)
Answer: pine
13. The city of Jericho was named for and famous for what trees? (2 Chronicles 28:15)
Answer: palms
14. The wood for Noah's ark came from what tree? (Genesis 6:14)
Answer: cypress
15. What wild tree was to be grafted in? (Romans 11:24)
Answer: olive
16. The angel of the Lord stood among what kind of trees? (Zechariah 1:11)
Answer: myrtle
17. What three kinds of trees were used to burn incense under because they cast such good shadows? (Hosea 4:13)
Answer: oak, poplar, terebrinth

18. The branches of what trees were cut and waved as the people went forth to meet Jesus? (John 12:13)
Answer: palm
19. What trees did Solomon ask for, and Hiram gave, for the construction of the Temple? (1 Kings 5:6)
Answer: cedars of Lebanon
20. What tree sprang from the wall? (1 Kings 4:33)
Answer: hyssop

Twig Weaving

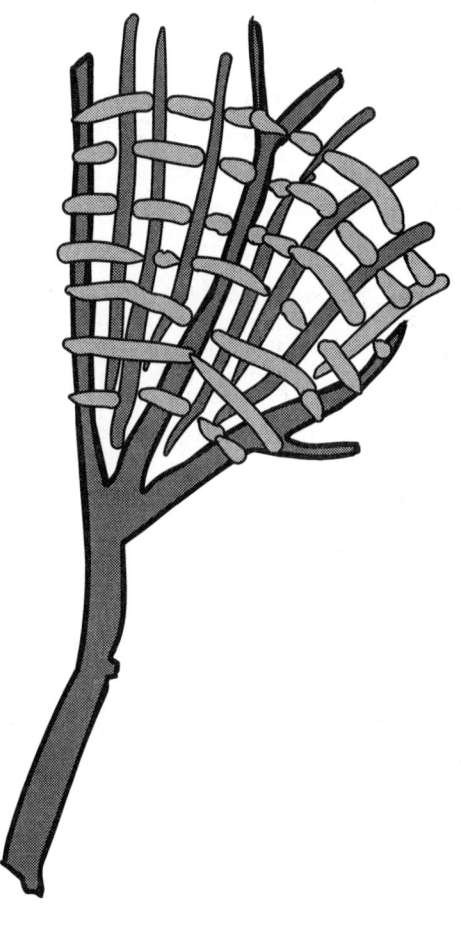

 Objective
To help children understand that they need to root themselves solidly in the Word of God in order to live righteous and holy lives

 Memory Verse
If the root is holy, so are the branches.
Romans 11:16

 Prayer
Dear God, we will trust in You to help us have deep and strong roots. Help us understand the Bible so that we will know what You want us to do. Amen.

Teach
Read the memory verse and discuss with the children what happens to plants that are not rooted properly — they are easily torn from the ground and destroyed. Those with solid roots grow tall and strong and produce fruit according to their purpose. The twig weaving below will help children remember this Scripture lesson.

You Will Need
• forked tree branches
• yarn or raffia
• grasses and weeds

Before Class
You may want to take the children on a nature hike to find the forked branches needed or you may ask them to look for some on their own and bring them to class. You will also want the children to collect many different kinds of grasses, weeds, leaves, etc., to use in their weavings.

What to Do
1. Show how to tie one end of the yarn or raffia to the top of one of the forks of the branch.
2. Have the students stretch the yarn across to the other fork, and wrap it around once.
3. Then they should stretch the yarn back across to the first fork, about 1/4" below the first wrap (where the knot is) and wrap the yarn around.
4. Have the children continue taking the yarn back and forth between the forks, wrapping it each time, until they reach the bottom of the fork.
5. Now instruct the students to weave the other materials (grasses, weeds, leaves, etc.) up and down through the yarn, going over one strand of yarn, then under the next, then over, and so on. Between the strands of yarn they can place seashells, mosses or other things too short to weave.

Twig Wreath

 Objective
To help children understand that God is the Great Creator whose reign is without end

 Memory Verse
He sits enthroned above the circle of the earth…
He stretches out the heavens like a canopy.
Isaiah 40:22

 Prayer
Dear God, help us to always keep You in our hearts and minds and to know that You will live in and love us forever. Amen.

Teach
Discuss with the children that God has been, is, and will be alive forever and forever — just like a circle, He has no end. To help remember this, have the children make circular twig wreathes to hang in their homes.

You Will Need
- wire hangers
- scissors
- green floral wire
- twigs
- tacky glue
- small pine cones, dried flowers or artificial decorations

Before Class
Untwist the handles of the hangers, bend the ends into a circle, and retwist them closed. Cut several pieces of wire about 6" long for each child. Green floral wire, available in craft stores, is excellent, but any fine-gauge wire will work. Be sure to instruct the children to bring twigs to class.

What to Do
1. Show how to take a handful of twigs and form them into a bunch.
2. Demonstrate how to wrap a piece of wire around the bunch at one end, and twist the ends of the wire together so the twigs stay together.
3. When each child has made several bunches, show how to start the wreath. Hold a bunch against the coat hanger circle and attach it with another piece of wire.
4. Add a second bunch of twigs, overlapping the wired ends of the first.
5. Keep adding bunches of twigs until the coat hanger is covered.
6. With tacky glue, show how to glue on small or medium-size pine cones, dried flowers and berries or artificial decorations. Let the glue dry.
7. Say, **Hang the wreath in remembrance of God's love for us forever.**

Types of Soil

Objective
To teach children that just as a house needs a good, solid foundation, so do our lives

Memory Verse
Therefore everyone who hears these words of mine and puts them into practice is like a wise man who built his house on the rock. But everyone who hears these words of mine and does not put them into practice is like a foolish man who built his house on sand. **Matthew 7:24, 26**

Prayer
Dear God, we need Your Word to be in our hearts so that we can build a solid foundation for our lives. Thank You for the Bible and for the Holy Spirit to help us learn and remember. Amen.

Teach
Say, **The earth is made up of many different types of matter — rock, pebbles, clay, sand, etc. — and each was created for a particular purpose…just like us!** The activity below is an easy way to see some of the different soil particles in order to give the students an idea of what they are.

You Will Need
- tall jars with screw caps
- soil
- water

What to Do
1. Give each child a jar.
2. Show how to scoop soil into the jar until it is about one-third full.
3. Help the students add water, but leave a 1" air space at the top.
4. Instruct the children to put on the caps and shake hard to mix the water and soil.
5. Have them put the jars down and watch the particles settle from the muddy water.
6. Ask, **Can you see different layers? The heaviest pebbles will be on the bottom, with sand next, and silt on top. Take off the cap. What is floating on the surface of the water? The smallest particles, clay, take longer to settle. The cloudy water should clear up in a day or two. When this happens, look for a very thin layer of clay on top of the silt.**
7. Discuss uses for the various parts of soil. Also discuss the importance of having a solid foundation in Christ and what people need to do to have one (pray, read the Bible, fellowship with other Christians, etc.).

Animal Adventures

A Little Birdie Told Them 52

Birds in the Bible Crossword. 53

Blowfish 55

Hiding Places 57

Nature's Intricacies 58

Worm Houses 60

God made the beasts.
Genesis 1:25 KJV

A Little Birdie Told Them

 Objective
To help children learn about God's love and care by how He created and used birds

 Memory Verse
You will drink from the brook, and I have ordered the ravens to feed you there. So he did what the Lord had told him. He went to the Kerith Ravine, east of the Jordan, and stayed there. The ravens brought him bread and meat in the morning and bread and meat in the evening, and he drank from the brook. **1 Kings 17:4-6**

 Prayer
Dear God, You have a purpose for everything You created. Please help me find Your purpose for my life. Thank You. Amen.

Teach
Use the quiz below as a Scripture hunt to see who can find the answer first. Or divide the class into teams to work together finding the answers. Give each team a different question.

Birds of the Bible
Besides the raven that fed Elijah, other well-known birds are mentioned in Scripture. With what event or teaching is each of these birds associated?

Which Bird:
Proved that the Flood had receded? (Genesis 8:11)
Answer: dove

Showed God's love for even the lowliest creatures? (Matthew 10:29)
Answer: sparrows

Was sacrificed when Jesus was presented in the temple as a baby? (Luke 2:21-24)
Answer: doves

Represent unlimited strength? (Isaiah 40:31)
Answer: eagles

Was sent to provide meat for the complaining Israelites? (Exodus 16:12-13)
Answer: quail

Was one of the birds forbidden as food under Old Testament laws? The screech _____ (Leviticus 11:16)
Answer: owl

Is the one that those who hope in the Lord and renew their strength will soar on wings of? (Isaiah 40:31)
Answer: eagles

Birds in the Bible Crossword

Objective
To increase awareness of how God uses nature to illustrate His truths

Memory Verse
Blessed is he whose help is the God of Jacob, whose hope is in the Lord his God, the Maker of heaven and earth, the sea, and everything in them the Lord, who remains faithful forever.
Psalm 146:5-6

Prayer
Dear God, thank You for making the birds of every color and shape just like You made Your children. We love You. Amen.

Teach

Discuss how God cares for the little birds, and how He cares for us much more. Then give each child a copy of page 54 and say, **You can solve this puzzle by fitting the words in the list below into the spaces on the diagram. Look up the scripture references to find which birds fit into which squares. Several of the references are the same. You will have to read the verse, see how many letters are needed to fill the corresponding spaces on the puzzle, then choose the correct bird for your answer.**

Birds In The Bible

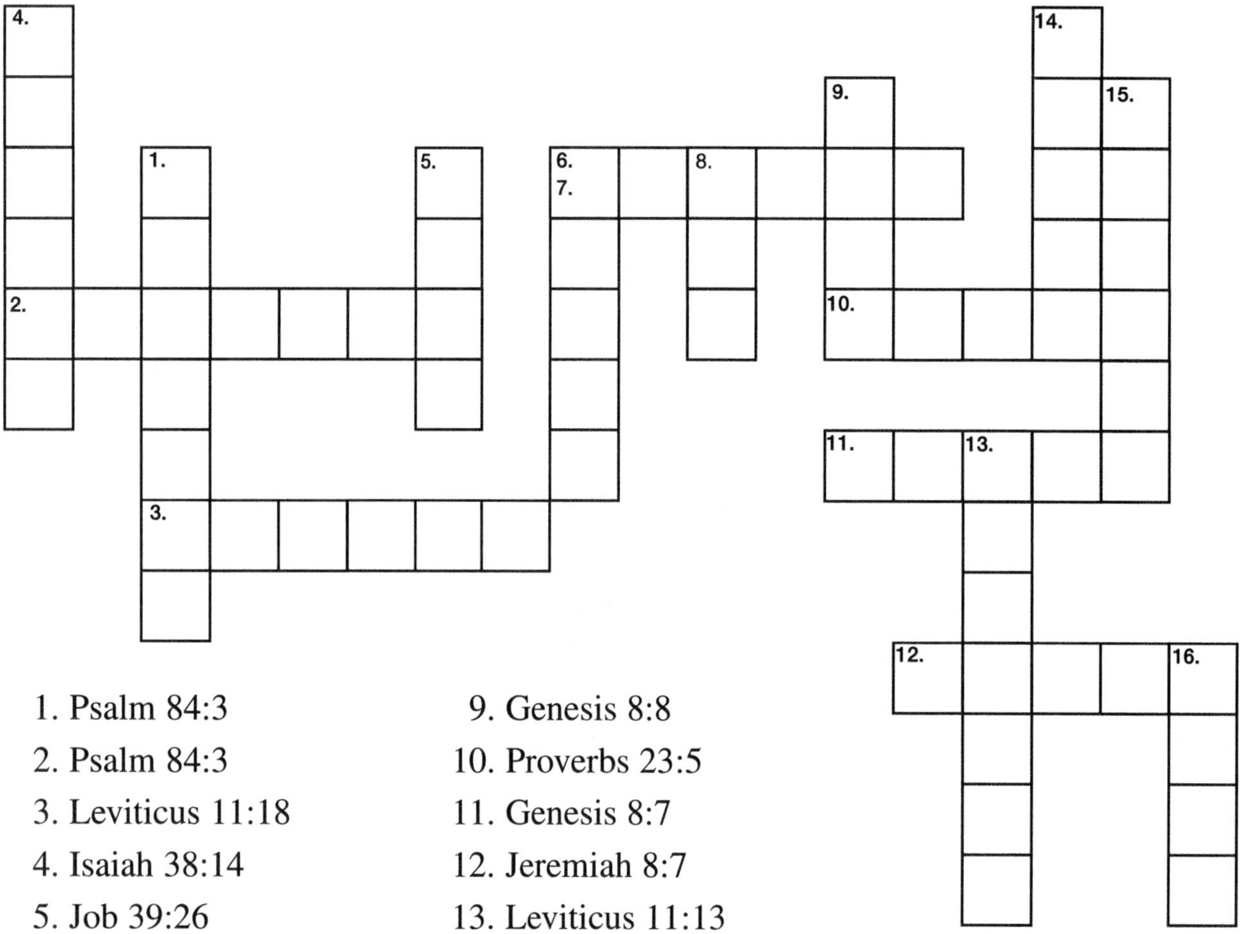

1. Psalm 84:3
2. Psalm 84:3
3. Leviticus 11:18
4. Isaiah 38:14
5. Job 39:26
6. Leviticus 11:19
7. Leviticus 11:19
8. Psalm 102:6
9. Genesis 8:8
10. Proverbs 23:5
11. Genesis 8:7
12. Jeremiah 8:7
13. Leviticus 11:13
14. Exodus 16:13
15. Leviticus 12:6
16. Leviticus 11:14

Answer Key

Blowfish

Objective
To help children realize the extent and beauty of creation

Memory Verse
And God said, "Let the water teem with living creatures." **Genesis 1:20**

Prayer
Dear God, thank You for the beauty of Your Creation, and for making so many, many different kinds of creatures for us to enjoy. Amen.

Teach
Say, **God created the birds that fly in the sky, and we see them daily as they rise and swoop through the air. He also created the fish that live deep in the waters of streams, rivers, lakes and oceans. We don't see fish often, unless we go to an aquarium. Then we see hundreds of different kinds, colors and sizes of fish…aren't they beautiful and graceful as they swim against the current of the water? God must certainly love beautiful things, for His creation is so full of beauty.**

You Will Need
- pattern on page 56
- tissue paper
- pencils
- scissors
- paint or markers
- glue
- plastic drinking straws
- tape
- string
- paint smocks

What to Do
1. Have each child place two sheets of tissue paper together and use the template to draw a fish shape on the tissue. Be sure they write lightly so as not to tear the tissue.
2. Instruct the students to cut out the fish.
3. Allow the children to use tempera or watercolor paint (have them wear paint smocks) or felt-tip markers to decorate their fish shapes.
4. Have each child glue together the two pieces, placing the glue only around the edges. Explain that they should leave a small opening at the mouth of the fish.
5. When the glue has dried, have the children insert straws into their fish and puff them up by blowing air into the straws.
6. After they remove the straws, they should quickly seal the opening with tape.
7. Hang the blowfish throughout the classroom by taping string to each one.

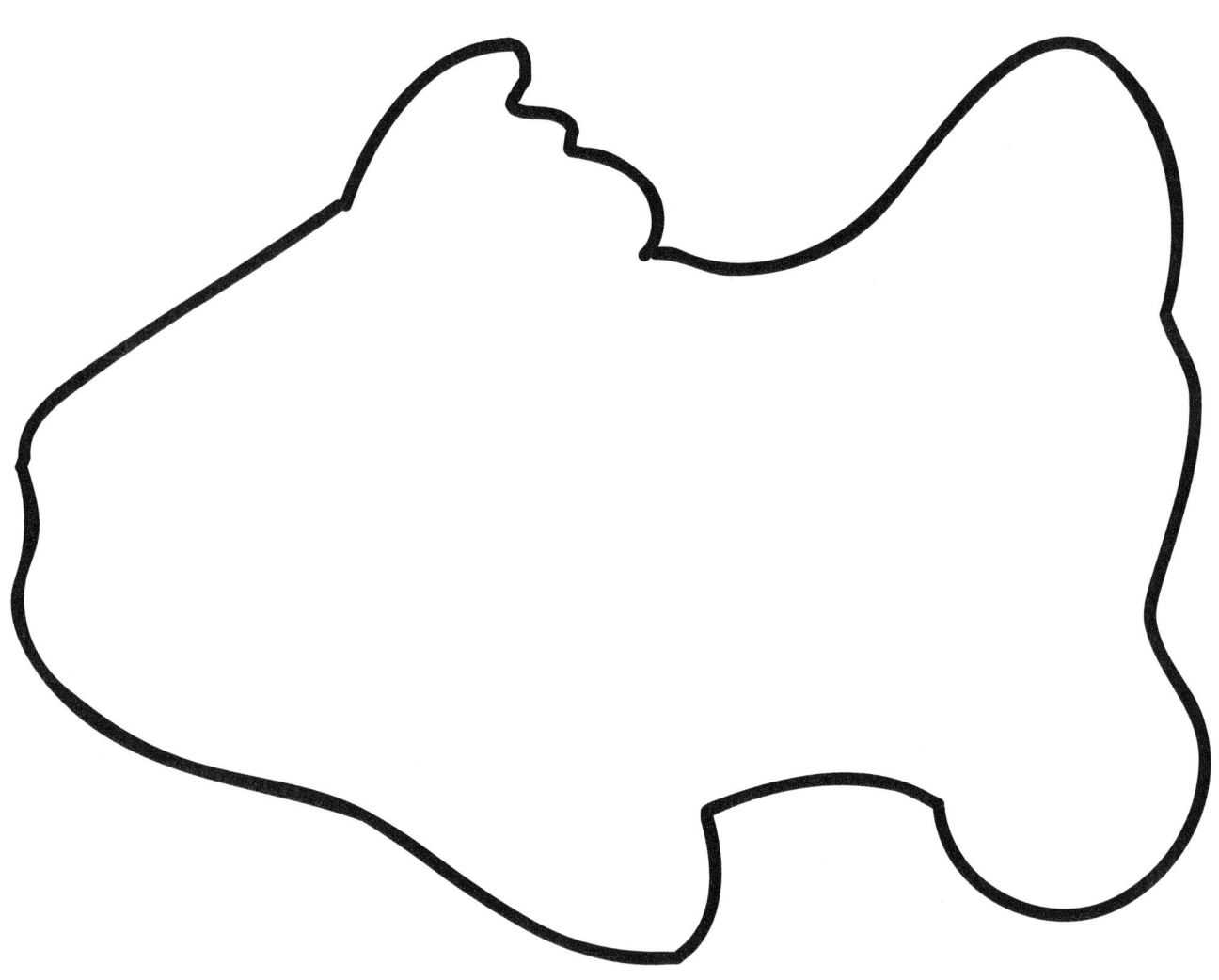

Hiding Places

Objective

To help children realize that just as God provides protection for things in nature, He will provide protection for us if we follow His will and call upon Him

Memory Verse

Keep me as the apple of your eye; hide me in the shadow of your wings from the wicked who assail me. **Psalm 17:8-9**

Prayer

Dear God, thank You for providing hiding places for protection of things in nature, and thank You for offering a hiding place from my enemies for me. Amen.

Teach

Say, **Some animals live inside shells that protect their soft bodies. The shells are usually hard and can be found in all sizes and colors. Shells found near the sea are generally made of a mineral called calcium. They no longer have an animal inside. You can file away the outer part of the shell to see the animal's home inside. It usually will have a spiral shape. As the animal or organism grew, it added layers to the shell, which appear as rings on the outside of the shell.**

What to Do

1. Use spiral shells (craft stores usually carry a supply of shells, but if you live near a beach, a nature search may be a good idea for the children).
2. Have several sheets of coarse sandpaper for the children to use.
3. Grip the shells tightly and rub them against the sandpaper
4. Continue to rub the shells to wear away one side.
5. Ask, **What do you see?** (Allow the children to respond).
6. Say, **God protects us like these shells protect animals. But His protection cannot be sanded away — He is always with us.**

Nature's Intricacies

 Objective
To help children look for beauty in all of nature

 Memory Verse
He has made everything beautiful in its time.
Ecclesiastes 3:11

 Prayer
Thank You, dear God, for the way You take care of everything that You created. And thank You for loving and taking care of us. Amen.

Teach

Say, **Often we shy away from some aspects of nature because of fear or apprehension. But then we do not have opportunities to see just how beautiful and intricate some of God's creations can be. Spider webs might be one of those things you fear. However, a web is simply a home for one of God's creations. God cares for even the tiniest of creatures…and He certainly cares for us.**

You Will Need

- page 59
- crayons

Before Class

Duplicate page 59 for each child.

What to Do

1. Give each child a copy of page 59.
2. Say, **You can use these directions to preserve a spider web that you find.** Briefly explain the directions.
3. Allow the children to color the sheet and take it home.

Spider webs can be collected to study by a simple procedure. When you see a spider web on a tree or fence, spray it with spray paint (ask an adult to help you and be careful not to get any on the fence). Then slip a piece of construction paper (contrasting color to that of the paint used) behind it and draw the paper slowly toward the web until the web is "captured" by the paper. The paint will cause the web to stick to the paper. These can be hung for display.

He has made everything beautiful in its time.
Ecclesiastes 3:11

Worm Houses

Objective
To help children realize that we don't always see everything taking place in nature the same as we don't always see God working in our lives, but we know He is there

Memory Verse
Look at the birds of the air; they do not sow or reap or store away in barns, and yet your heavenly Father feeds them. Are you not much more valuable than they? **Matthew 6:26**

Prayer
Dear God, thank You for Your promise to take care of us and provide for our needs. Help us to learn to trust You in all areas of our life. Thank You. Amen.

Teach
Say, **God gave worms to help prepare soil and keep it soft for seeds to grow. God is working where we cannot see. Often in our own lives we need help to make our pathway smooth. God is always at work to direct our steps even though we do not always see Him. We trust that He will do what He has said in the Bible and care for us and guide us.**

You Will Need
- clear glass jar
- soil
- tree leaves
- cabbage leaves
- coffee grounds
- $1/2$ teaspoon brown sugar
- earthworms
- water
- dark paper

What to Do
1. In a large clear glass jar place the following in layers: soil, tree leaves, cabbage leaves, coffee grounds and $1/2$ teaspoon brown sugar.
2. Finish with a thin layer of soil on top, then place a few earthworms on top of the soil.
3. Sprinkle a little water on top.
4. Cover the sides of the jar with dark paper to keep light from them.
5. After a few days, take the paper off and observe with the children what has happened. The worms will have made tunnels through the mixture. Some of the tunnels may be visible along the sides of the jar.
6. Add a little water, brown sugar, and cabbage leaves periodically. Keep the dark paper on the sides of the jar except when you are observing the worms.

Outdoor Observations

Crazy Clouds 62

God Is Faithful Nature Pantomime 63

Make a Rainbow 63

God's Control of Seasons 64

God's Gift of Weather 69

Making Rain 72

Raindrop Preservation 73

Shadow Clock 74

Star Gaze 75

Star-Studded Peep Boxes. 76

Static Electricity 77

The Seasons Table Scene 78

Wind Speed 80

You know how to interpret...the sky.
Matthew 16:3

Crazy Clouds

 Objective
To encourage children to think of ways the heavens show the glory of God

 Memory Verse
The heavens proclaim his righteousness, and all the peoples see his glory. **Psalm 97:6**

 Prayer
Dear God, we love to look at the heavens You created and see the beautiful white fluffy clouds as well as the dark and stormy ones. You have given us so many wonderful kinds of clouds to see. Thank You. Amen.

Teach
Read aloud Psalm 97:6. Encourage the children to think of some ways that the heavens show the glory of God.

You Will Need
- blue construction paper
- white chalk or crayons
- felt-tip pen or dark crayon

Before Class
Write the memory verse at the bottom of each child's sheet.

What to Do
1. Give each child a sheet of blue construction paper and white chalk or a crayon to draw clouds.
2. When everyone has completed their pictures, discuss how beautiful clouds are. Also talk about how, with a little imagination, clouds can look like many things.
3. Have each child take a felt-tip pen or crayon and, using his or her imagination, create a picture out of the clouds.
4. Ask the students to share the pictures with one another.

God Is Faithful Nature Pantomime

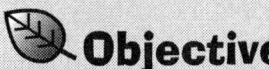 Objective
To help children appreciate the faithfulness of God, which is so evident in the world He has created

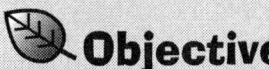 Memory Verse
I will sing of the Lord's great love forever; with my mouth I will make your faithfulness known through all generations. **Psalm 89:1**

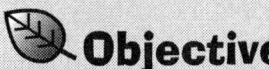 Prayer
Thank You, God, for Your faithfulness that we see in nature and how You are constantly present and caring for Your creation and us. Amen.

Teach
Divide the children into four groups: spring, summer, winter and autumn. Have each group plan a short pantomime that portray activities for their season, such as planting a garden or walking under umbrellas, swimming or boating, raking leaves or picking apples, putting on winter clothes or shoveling snow. As each group performs their pantomime, encourage the others to guess what they are doing.

Make a Rainbow

 Objective
To show how God used nature to promise His love

 Memory Verse
I have set my rainbow in the clouds, and it will be the sign of the covenant between me and the earth. **Genesis 9:13**

 Prayer
Dear God, thank You for Your promise of love, and thank You for Your beautiful rainbows that we love to see in the sky. Each time we see one we are drawn closer to You and love You more. Amen.

Teach
Make a rainbow! You need a glass of water and a sunny day. For best results, use a clear glass with a wide mouth. Take the class outside and place the glass in sunlight. Have everyone look for a rainbow where the shadow would fall (what you have made is a simple prism that reflects the color spectrum). Ask the children to tell you the Bible story that has a rainbow in it (Genesis 6-9).

God's Control of Seasons

Objective
To help children appreciate the fact that God makes all kinds of weather and controls it

Memory Verse
He loads the clouds with moisture; he scatters his lightning through them. At his direction they swirl around over the face of the whole earth to do whatever he commands them. **Job 37:11-12**

Prayer
Dear God, thank You for giving us seasons and different kinds of weather and thank You for being in control of it. You are a great and wonderful God. Amen.

Teach

Photocopy or remove pages 65-68 and color the pictures. Divide the classroom into four areas and post a sign in each section. As the children enter the room, have them go to the area that features the season in which their birthdays occur. There should be a leader in each section of the room to guide the discussion and activities. Each group may discuss the kind of weather that comes during "their" season. For example, ask, **Are most days long or short in the summer? What can we do in the summer that we cannot do in winter? What happens to trees in the autumn? What kinds of weather do we have? Are days long or short in the winter?**

What to Do

1. Have the children prepare a short pantomime suggesting seasonal weather activities, such as planting a garden, swimming, or raking leaves.
2. Write Genesis 8:22 on the chalkboard and read it aloud: "As long as the earth endures, seedtime and harvest, cold and heat, summer and winter, day and night will never cease."
3. Ask, **Who controls the weather?**

Spring
March 21 to June 20

Summer
June 21 to September 22

Autumn
September 23 to December 21

Winter
December 22 to March 20

God's Gift of Weather

🍃 Objective
To help children realize God's power

🍃 Memory Verse
He makes clouds rise from the ends of the earth. He sends lightning with the rain and brings out the wind from his storehouses.
Jeremiah 10:13

🍃 Prayer
Thank You, God, for making so many different kinds of weather. You know exactly what we need at all times. Amen.

Teach

Lead a discussion about wind and rain, letting the children contribute as much as they can. Ask, **What is wind?** (moving air) **Why does the wind blow?** (Warm air is lighter than cold air and will rise above it. The movement causes wind.) **What good things does wind do?** (carries seeds, cools us, dries things) **Who controls the wind?** (God) If any child mentions disasters brought about by wind, agree that this happens. However, emphasize that God takes care of His children and always knows what is best for them — even death, which seems bad, but brings believing Christians home to Him. Continue asking questions. **Why does it rain?** (The drops of water in clouds grow heavy enough to drop to the ground.) **How do clouds get water in them?** (Water on earth evaporates into the air. Warm air carries the water vapor up where it cools. As it cools, it forms droplets, which gather together and make a cloud.)

You Will Need
• pages 70 and 71

Before Class
Duplicate pages 70 and 71 for each child (back-to-back if possible). You may use this activity in-class or as a take-home paper.

What to Do
1. Give each child a copy of pages 70-71.
2. Help the students write in the dates of the month on both sides.
3. Tell the children that each day they should see what God is sending in His weather and draw a picture on that date on the Today's Weather calendar….a sun, rain, wind, snow flakes, clouds, etc. They should also write the high and low temperatures for each day.
4. On the My Weather side, encourage the students to write a note for each day telling how they felt about the weather or how the weather made them feel.
5. At the end of the month, ask the children to bring their calendars back to class for comparison.

Today's Weather

Month: _____

Sunday	Monday	Tuesday	Wednesday	Thursday	Friday	Saturday

He loads the clouds with moisture; he scatters his lightning through them. At his direction they swirl around over the face of the whole earth to do whatever he commands them. Job 37:11-12

My Weather

Month: _____

Sunday	Monday	Tuesday	Wednesday	Thursday	Friday	Saturday

He loads the clouds with moisture; he scatters his lightning through them. At his direction they swirl around over the face of the whole earth to do whatever he commands them. Job 37:11-12

Making Rain

 Objective
To help children understand that God made nature to act in certain ways and nature obeys His commands just as we should

 Memory Verse
Be glad, O people of Zion, rejoice in the Lord your God...He sends you abundant showers, both autumn and spring rains. **Joel 2:23**

 Prayer
Thank You, dear God, for giving us rain, and for giving us rules to follow. Help us to be obedient. Amen.

Teach
Say, **Water is created and moves in cycles. When it rains, water falls and soaks into the earth or runs into waterways. When water on the earth is heated, it turns into water vapor and is carried around in the air. The water partially evaporates. This vapor condenses in the atmosphere and forms clouds, which produce rain.** Try this experiment with the students to make your own rain.

You Will Need
- plastic sandwich bags
- soil
- water
- tape

Before Class
You will need one zip-type plastic sandwich bag for each child.

What to Do
1. Give each child a plastic sandwich bag.
2. Show how to place a small amount of soil in the bottom of the plastic bag.
3. Help the students sprinkle just enough tap water on the soil to dampen it.
4. Instruct the children to close the bags so they are tight and tape them to a sunny window.
5. Say, **Let's observe the bags for the a while. What is happening?** As the sun warms the soil in the bags, water droplets will form at the tops. When enough water collects at the top, it will become heavy and fall back to the soil like rain.

Raindrop Preservation

 Objective
To help children realize that God takes care of those who love Him and will provide our needs

 Memory Verse
If you follow my decrees and are careful to obey my commands, I will send you rain in its season, and the ground will yield its crops and the trees of the field their fruit. **Leviticus 26:3-4**

 Prayer
Dear God, thank You for knowing what I need and for providing for my needs. Amen.

Teach
Ask, **Have you ever thought about saving a raindrop? Have you even thought such a thing was possible? Well, let's find out!** Have the children assist you in making the raindrops.

You Will Need
- permanent marker
- flour
- baking pan
- slotted spoon
- oven
- small containers

Before Class
Write the memory verse on the outside of a small, clear container for each child.

What to Do
1. Spread flour in a baking pan so it is about 1" thick.
2. Take the pan outside and hold it in the rain.
3. After several raindrops fall onto the flour, bring the pan inside.
4. Sift out the floured raindrops with a slotted spoon.
5. Empty the excess flour from the pan, then place the wet flour pieces in the baking pan.
6. Bake the raindrops at 350 degrees until they are hard.
7. After baking, the flour will harden and create a raindrop model. Give each student a few baked raindrops in a container.
8. Say, **Place your raindrops where you can see them as a reminder that God will supply your needs just as our memory verse tells us.**

Shadow Clock

 Objective
To show how God made the sun to be a clock and to move across the heavens to bring light and darkness

 Memory Verse
Give thanks to the Lord, for he is good. His love endures forever. Who made the great lights — His love endures forever. The sun to govern the day, His love endures forever. The moon and stars to govern the night; His love endures forever.
Psalm 136:1, 7-9

 Prayer
Dear God, thank You for the sun that gives us light, and for Your wonderful plan of creation. Amen.

Teach
Say, **People in biblical times used clocks like we are going to make, clocks that told time by the placement of shadows. They told time by using the sun as a clock. A person watched his shadow grow longer and longer. Today our clocks lets us know when it is time to stop work or school and go home. In Bible times when a person was tired and wanted to go home from work, he'd say, "How long my shadow is in coming!"**

You Will Need
- pencils
- paper plates
- crayons

What to Do
1. On a bright sunny day at the beginning of class time, show the children how to push a pencil halfway through a paper plate.
2. Go outside and have them poke the pencil in the ground. The pencil will make a shadow on the plate.
3. Have the students make a mark where the shadow falls. Leave the plates for an hour and return inside.
4. When you come back out, ask, **Where is the shadow? The sun has moved, time has passed.**

Star Gaze

Objective
To bring awareness of the powerfulness of God

Memory Verse
When I consider your heavens, the work of your fingers, the moon and the stars, which you have set in place. **Psalm 8:3**

Prayer
Dear God, we are so small in the great big universe You have created, yet You know us and love us very much. Thank You. We love You, too, and are amazed at all that You can do. Amen.

Teach
Read Psalm 8 to the class. Ask, **What do you think about a God so powerful that He could create billions of stars and yet be so personal that He knows and cares for each child?** Have a circle of prayer thanking God for His power and love.

You Will Need
- round oatmeal containers
- needle
- flashlight

Before Class
Use a needle to make holes in the shape of one of the constellations, such as the Big Dipper, in the bottom of an oatmeal container. Make several of the constellation boxes to show the different star formations.

What to Do
1. Make your room as dark as possible.
2. Remove the lid and insert a flashlight.
3. Shine the flashlight through the box onto the ceiling of the room to see the stars "shine."
4. Ask if the children can identify the constellations as they appear.
5. Talk about the beauty of the universe and the great God who put the stars in place.

Star-Studded Peep Boxes

Objective

To help children realize God's love by learning that He knows the names of all the stars in the heavens and He knows our names, too

Memory Verse

He determines the number of the stars and calls them each by name. Great is our Lord and mighty in power; his understanding has no limit.
Psalm 147:4-5

Prayer

Thank You, dear God, for placing the beautiful shining stars in the heavens and for knowing each of their names. Also, thank You for knowing our names. Help us to remember how great You are each time we look at the stars in the sky. Amen.

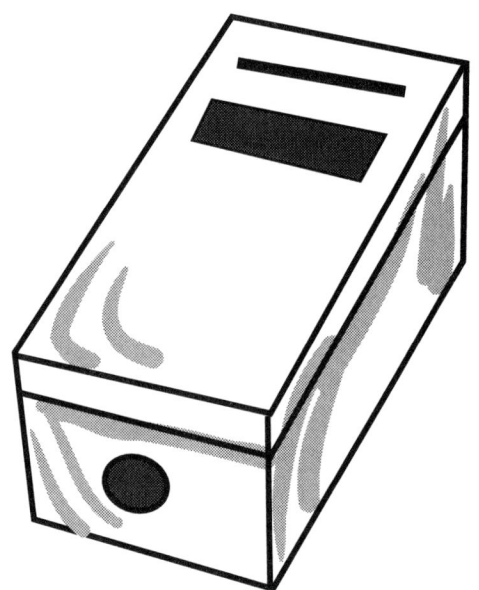

Teach

Say, **God put some of the stars into groups to make pictures.** Show illustrations of the constellations. Ask if the children can tell what the pictures are. Discuss the names of the constellations. Say, **We can use peep boxes to bring the constellations right into our rooms or homes.**

You Will Need

- shoe boxes
- small paper stars
- blue construction paper
- black felt-tip pen
- silver stars
- encyclopedia
- pins
- scissors

Before Class

Cut a hole about the size of a half-dollar on one end of each shoe box to serve as a peep-hole. At the opposite end on the lid, show how to cut out a rectangle to allow light to enter the box. Beyond this opening, closer to the edge, cut a slit slightly wider than five inches. Cut one box for each child. Cut the blue construction paper into one 3" x 5" piece for each child.

What to Do

1. Look up the major constellations in an encyclopedia or book about stars. Either draw the constellations on the chalkboard or place the book where the children can easily see it.
2. Allow the students to select a constellation.
3. Give each child a cut piece of blue construction paper and have them draw a constellation on it, marking the locations of the stars.
4. Instruct the children to glue silver stars in the correct places.
5. Show how to make a tiny hole in the center of each star with a pin.
6. Have them write the name of the constellation along the top.
7. Give each child a pre-cut shoe box.
8. Show how to slide the card through the slit in the lid. As they look through the peep hole the light will shine through, illuminating the stars and outlining the constellation.

Static Electricity

 Objective
To help children realize the vastness of nature and how the various elements work together

 Memory Verse
Praise the Lord from the earth, you great sea creatures and all ocean depths, lightning and hail, snow and clouds, stormy winds that do his bidding. **Psalm 148:7-8**

 Prayer
Thank You, God, for letting us have fun with Your creation of static electricity. You are indeed a great and awesome God. We love You. Amen.

Teach
Say, **Static electricity is interesting to watch. God makes the electricity in the skies when lightning happens during a storm, but we can make electricity right in the classroom.**

You Will Need
- box with a plastic lid
- puffed rice cereal
- tissue paper
- wool cloth
- comb
- inflated balloon
- nylon, silk or cotton thread

What to Do
1. Have the children place a handful of puffed rice and bits of tissue in the box with a plastic lid.
2. Let them take turns rubbing the plastic with their hand or a piece of wool and watch the objects dance in the box and cling to the lid.
3. Allow the children to rub the balloon against their clothing or hair then touch it to the wall and watch it stick.
4. Show how to hold the balloon over your head so your hair stands on end!
5. Charge a comb by rubbing it on wool.
6. Cut some pieces of nylon, silk or cotton thread, making some of the threads short and some long.
7. Move the comb near the threads.
8. Say, **God must have a good sense of humor to let us have fun making static electricity!**

The Seasons Table Scene

 Objective
To show how God makes nature grow and renew by changing seasons

 Memory Verse
As long as the earth endures, seedtime and harvest, cold and heat, summer and winter, day and night will never cease. **Genesis 8:22**

 Prayer
Dear God, spring, summer, fall and winter are each so beautiful and useful in their own ways. Thank You for planning and making our world to change and grow in such a beautiful way. Amen.

Teach
Discuss what happens in nature as the seasons change. Ask, **How do you feel as the seasons change?** Give thanks to God for His wisdom in creating the different seasons.

You Will Need
- page 79
- crayons

Before Class
Duplicate page 79 for each child.

What to Do
1. Give each child a copy of page 79.
2. Have each child select a "symbol" for nature, then draw it as it is affected by each season. For example, for spring a tree would have blossoms on it; for summer the tree would be green; for autumn the tree would have multicolored leaves and for winter the tree would be bare.
3. Place on a table as a centerpiece or table placemat.

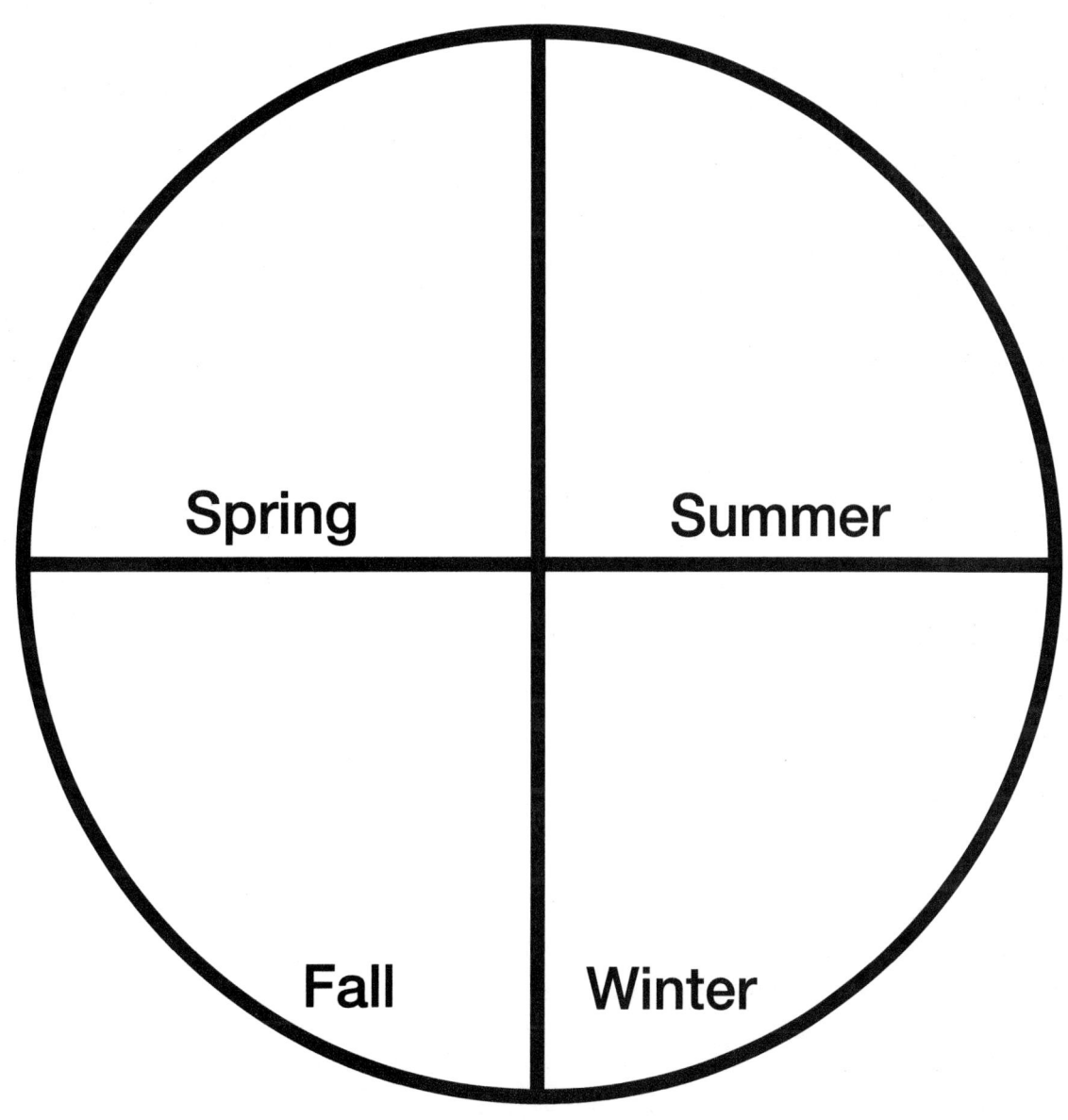

Wind Speed

Objective
To help children realize that God not only created the world and all that is in it, He has total control over it

Memory Verse
Even the wind and the waves obey him! **Mark 4:41**

Prayer
Dear God, thank You for the gentle breezes and for the strong storms. Help us to trust in You that You will be with us through any storm we face in life. Amen.

Teach

Review the story of Jesus calming the winds in Mark 4:35-41. Then say, **God created the wind for many different purposes. A soft gentle breeze cools the earth. A moderate wind scatters seeds and dries the earth from heavy rains. A strong wind sometimes causes great damage and brings changes that cause us to call upon God for His help.**

What to Do

1. Duplicate page 81 for each child.
2. The students can use the chart to determine wind speed.
3. Encourage them to check their estimates against what the local meteorologist says.

Less than 1 MPH (mile per hour): Mirror-still water surfaces. Smoke rises straight up from fires and chimneys.

1-3 MPH: Light air. Small ripples on lakes. You can tell wind direction by watching smoke as it drifts off. This wind will not register on weather vanes.

4-8 MPH: Light breeze. Wind can be felt on face. Leaves rustle. Weather vane moves.

9-12 MPH: Gentle breeze. Leaves and twigs in constant motion. Small, light flags are extended out from the pole.

13-18 MPH: Moderate breeze. Dust and paper blow before wind. Small branches move.

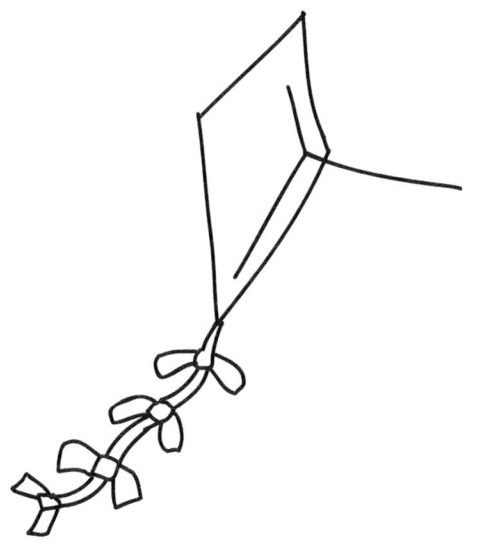

19-24 MPH: Fresh freeze. Small whitecaps. Small leafy trees sway.

25-31 MPH: Strong breeze. Large branches dance in the wind. Phone wires jump a little and may whistle. It is difficult to carry open umbrellas.

32-38 MPH: Moderate gale. Trees bend with the wind. It takes a little effort to walk into the wind.

39-46 MPH: Fresh gale. Twigs snap off trees. You have to hunch over and fight against a head wind to make progress.

47-54 MPH: Strong gale. Shingles blow off roofs.

55-63 MPH: Whole gale. Trees topple. Buildings are damaged.

64-72 MPH: Storm. Much damage.

73 MPH and up: Hurricane. Extreme damage.

The stronger the wind is, the shorter the length of time each gust will blow. As a gust of wind speeds up it moves clockwise (veering). As it slows down it moves counterclockwise (backing).

Even the wind and the waves obey him!
Mark 4:41

Food Fun

Fruits of the Spirit 85

God Gives Us Variety 87

Growing Vines 89

How Does Your Garden Grow? 91

Let's Paint Apples 92

Pomanders 93

Pumpkins and Leaves 95

Seeking Light 96

I am the bread of life. John 6:35

Fruits of the Spirit

🍃 Objective
To inspire children to trust in the Lord and to determine to live useful lives for Him

🍃 Memory Verse
Ah, Sovereign Lord, you have made the heavens and the earth by your great power and outstretched arm. Nothing is too hard for you. **Jeremiah 32:17**

🍃 Prayer
Dear God, thank You for being such a strong and faithful God. Help us to live for You in such a way that our lives will show the Fruits of the Spirit to others. Thank You. Amen.

Teach
Discuss the Fruits of the Spirit with the class and list them out. Explain why they are called "fruit." Refer to Galatians 5:22-23.

You Will Need
- page 86
- scissors
- crayons
- poster paper

Before Class
Duplicate page 86.

What to Do
1. Give each child a copy of page 86.
2. Have the children color and cut out the shapes.
3. Write the Fruits of the Spirit on chalkboard so the students can write them on the fruit shapes.
4. Have them glue the fruit to a larger sheet of paper for display in your classroom.

God Gives Us Variety

**Objective**
To help children realize their need to praise God for all that He has done for them through nature

**Memory Verse**
I will extol the Lord at all times; his praise will always be on my lips. **Psalm 34:1**

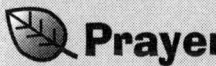**Prayer**
Thank You, Lord, for knowing all the things we need and for giving us enough variety to make our lives interesting. Amen.

Teach
Ask, **Wouldn't you get tired of eating the same thing meal after meal? What if the only food God created was carrots? We would have boiled carrots, glazed carrots, barbecued carrots, roasted carrots, mashed carrots, pureed carrots, sweet and sour carrots, carrot salad, carrot soup, carrot ice cream, carrot burgers, carrot milkshakes, deep fried carrots, etc. Or, what if we only had one kind of flower to look at? You get the idea. How grateful we should be that God actually created hundreds of kinds of food…there are hundreds of kinds of seeds that grow into food and flowers. God knew we needed variety and He always provides what we need.**

You Will Need
- page 88
- pencils
- seeds
- glue

Before Class
Duplicate page 88 for each child.

What to Do
1. Provide a variety of seeds for the children — as many different kinds as possible: orange, apple, cherry, peach, watermelon, grape, strawberry, celery, pumpkin, milkweed, burr, dandelion, pea, potato, marigold, poppy, petunia, carrot, radish, bean, avocado, etc. Have enough seeds so that each child can have one or two of each.
2. Give each child a copy of page 88. Let the children each take a sampling of the different seeds and glue them in the squares of their paper.
3. Have them write the name of each seed in the squares.
4. Ask each child to write a short prayer at the bottom of the paper thanking God for giving such a wonderful variety in nature.

God Gives Us Variety

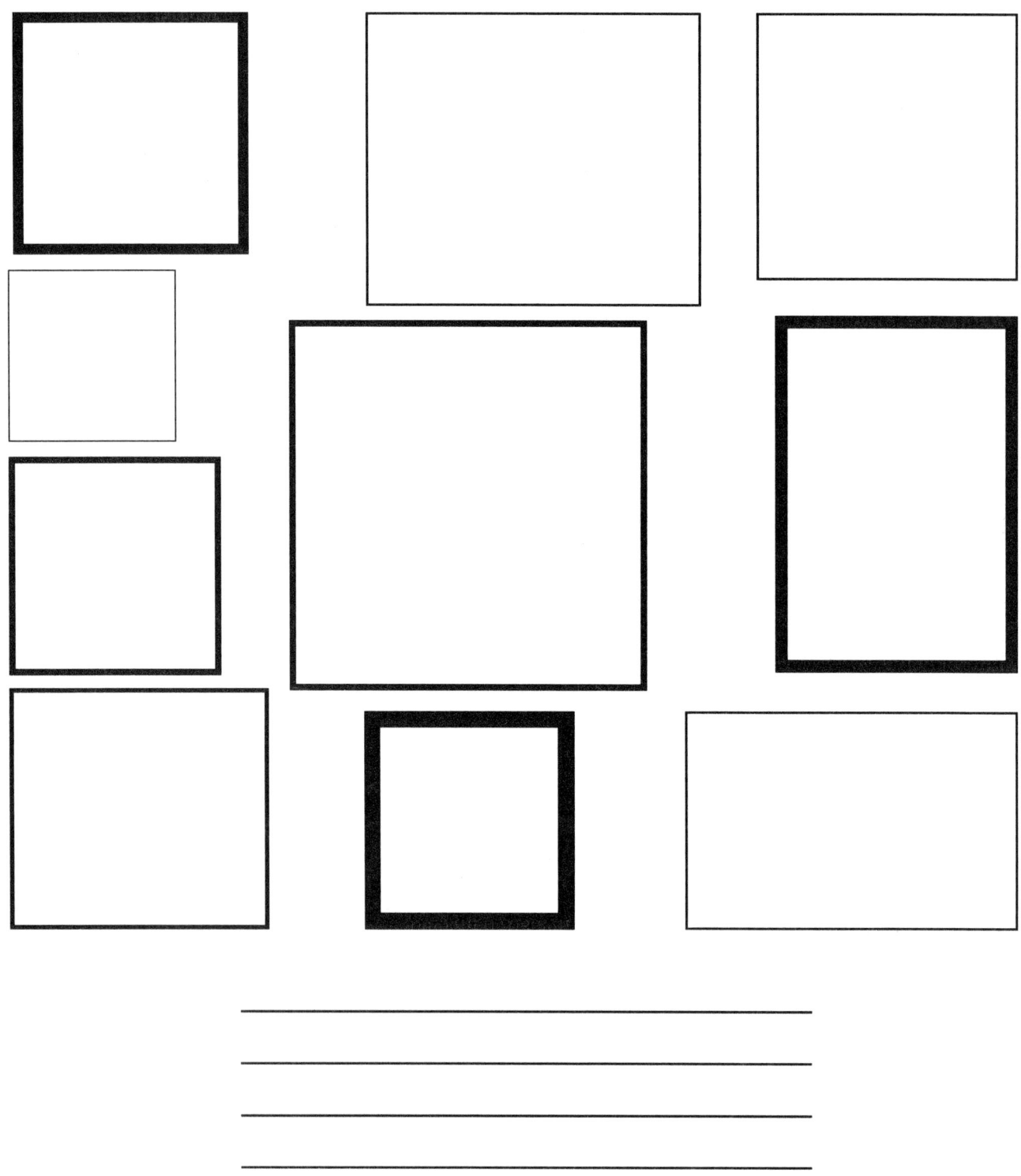

_____
_____
_____
_____

*I will extol the Lord at all times;
his praise will always be on my lips.* Psalm 34:1

Growing Vines

 ## Objective
To help children appreciate that God not only plants (creates), He cares for His creations (including each of us) and helps them become better, stronger and more fruitful

 ## Memory Verse
I am the true vine, and my Father is the gardener. He cuts off every branch in me that bears no fruit, while every branch that does bear fruit he prunes so that it will be even more fruitful. **John 15:1-2**

 ## Prayer
Thank You, God, for giving us Jesus, who is the True Vine that we can cling to. Please train us in the way we are to go. Amen.

Teach
Read the memory verse aloud. Then say, **Did you know that God is like a gardener? How do you think God is like a gardener?** (Allow the students to respond.) **God is like a gardener in our lives, helping us to get rid of our bad behavior and replacing it with good actions. And He does it gently, just like a gardener carefully prunes plants. That way we bear only fruit.**

You Will Need
- note from page 90
- small sweet potatoes
- jars
- toothpicks
- water

Before Class
Duplicate and cut out a note for each child's parents.

What to Do
1. Show how to poke three or four rounded toothpicks in a circle about one-third of the way from one end of a sweet potato.
2. Demonstrate how to submerge the potato into the jar — one-third in and two-thirds out.
3. Help the children fill their jars with water until it just covers the bottom tips of their potatoes.
4. Unless you meet more than weekly, you will want the children to take their potatoes home for observation and water. Give each child a duplicate note to explain the care and intent of the project to parents.

Dear Parents,

The potato your child is bringing home helps to illustrate the memory verse below about Jesus. We discussed how God is like a gardener in our lives, helping us to get rid of our bad behavior and replacing it with good actions.

For the vine to grow, choose a place near a window that faces the south in order to get the most sunshine. Keep the water touching the bottom tip until the potato sprouts. The jar will fill up with roots. Continue watering as long as the vine grows out of the top. Tie the vine to the wall to maintain its direction when it's long enough, keeping it in strong light from the south window.

_____
teacher

I am the true vine, and my Father is the gardener. He cuts off every branch in me that bears no fruit, while every branch that does bear fruit he prunes so that it will be even more fruitful.

— **John 15:1-2**

Dear Parents,

The potato your child is bringing home helps to illustrate the memory verse below about Jesus. We discussed how God is like a gardener in our lives, helping us to get rid of our bad behavior and replacing it with good actions.

For the vine to grow, choose a place near a window that faces the south in order to get the most sunshine. Keep the water touching the bottom tip until the potato sprouts. The jar will fill up with roots. Continue watering as long as the vine grows out of the top. Tie the vine to the wall to maintain its direction when it's long enough, keeping it in strong light from the south window.

_____
teacher

I am the true vine, and my Father is the gardener. He cuts off every branch in me that bears no fruit, while every branch that does bear fruit he prunes so that it will be even more fruitful.

— **John 15:1-2**

How Does Your Garden Grow?

Objective
To show how things of nature grow from seeds and to express awe over God's great plan for us

Memory Verse
He makes grass grow for the cattle, and plants for man to cultivate — bringing forth food from the earth. **Psalm 104:14**

Prayer
Dear God, thank You for providing all the things we need in life. Your plan of creation is awesome. We love You and thank You. Amen.

Teach
Say, **God had a wonderful plan for us when He made our great big world. There were so many things to think of and to plan for. How would we get food? How could we have something pretty to look at? God made seeds to grow so that we would have grains, vegetables, fruit and pretty flowers. But how do the seeds grow? Well, let's find out.**

You Will Need
- plastic sandwich bags
- paper towels
- seeds

Before Class
Large quick-sprouting seeds such as radish, peas or beans work best for this activity.

What to Do
1. Give each child a plastic sandwich bag, a damp paper towel and some seeds.
2. Show how to plant the garden by placing a damp paper towel and some seeds into a bag. They can choose various kinds of seeds to place in separate rows or different kinds in different bags.
3. Help the children seal the bags.
4. Arrange the bags on a shelf or in several shallow boxes.
5. The children may take the bags home so they can daily observe the process. Encourage them to check the seeds daily to see which ones sprout first. There is no need to rewater the toweling — if the bags are sealed, the towels will stay moist and the seeds will grow in about three weeks. After the seeds have grown about three inches tall, they may be transplanted outdoors or in indoor planters.

Let's Paint Apples

 ## Objective
To show the power of the sun and to teach how God gave the sun for us to grow properly

 ## Memory Verse
Give thanks to the Lord, for he is good, His love endures forever…who made the great lights — His love endures forever. The sun to govern the day, His love endures forever…and who gives food to every creature. His love endures forever.
Psalm 136:1, 7-8, 25

 ## Prayer
Dear God, thank You for the sun that You placed in the sky to give us light and warmth to help us grow. We love You. Amen.

Teach
Say, **Let's paint apples with the sun! The sun is like a big brush that paints — not on paper, but on plants. God gave the sun so that we would have warmth and nourishment to grow. With this experiment, we will see what happens when the sun is withheld from doing its work. The sun helps turn green leaves to red or yellow in the fall. And the sun paints many fruits a different color when they are ripe. The sun turns apples red when they are ripe, but only the side that is in the sun. The shaded side may still be yellow or green. But if you set the shaded side in the sun, it, too, will turn red.**

You Will Need
- red apples, partially unripened
- construction paper
- scissors
- tape

Before Class
Purchase red apples that are still partly green, one per child. Yellow apples that are not supposed to turn red will not work!

What to Do
1. Have the children cut the letters of their name or a simple shape from construction paper.
2. Show how to put the letters or shape on a piece of tape and stick the tape to the green side of an apple.
3. Help the students place the apples in a window so the sun will shine where the tape is.
4. In a few days, the green side will turn red.
5. At your next class, have the children remove the letters or shapes to reveal that the name or shape is still green.
6. Say, **The sun has painted the apple, except where it could not reach it under the tape. Give God thanks for the sun and what it does to make our lives healthy and happy.**

Pomanders

Objective
To help children realize that God covers His children with a holy fragrance that helps them live righteous lives

Memory Verse
Your God, has set you above your companions by anointing you with the oil of joy. **Psalm 45:7**

Prayer
Thank You, dear God, for giving us such wonderful-smelling spices. Anoint us with the holy fragrance of Your love and keep us in Your care. Amen.

Teach
Say, **Spices and various fragrances were used in Bible times to make precious perfumes and oils to anoint the tabernacles and the high priests. They were also used as gifts for very special occasions such as the gift of myrrh to baby Jesus by the wise men. We can also make a special gift of spices to give to a loved one. Pomanders can be placed in drawers or closets so they will smell good.**

You Will Need
- tag from page 94
- scissors
- crayons
- hole punch
- oranges
- whole cloves
- narrow ribbon
- nails

Before Class
You will need one orange, one ounce of cloves and two feet of narrow ribbon per child. Duplicate the memory verse tag from page 94 for each child.

What to Do
1. Have the children color and cut out the memory verse tag. Pass around a hole punch to make a hole where indicated.
2. Show how to thread the tag on the ribbon, then wrap the ribbon around the orange and tie a bow at the top. (You may need to provide a bit of tacky glue to hold the ribbon in place.)
3. Demonstrate how to use a nail to poke small holes in the orange and put a clove into each hole. Put the cloves as close together as possible.
4. Say, **Place your pomander in a cool, dark closet or drawer until it is hard and dry. It will shrink as it dries and will smell spicy and wonderful for years.**

Your God, has set you above your companions by anointing you with the oil of joy.
Psalm 45:7

Your God, has set you above your companions by anointing you with the oil of joy.
Psalm 45:7

Your God, has set you above your companions by anointing you with the oil of joy.
Psalm 45:7

Your God, has set you above your companions by anointing you with the oil of joy.
Psalm 45:7

Pumpkins and Leaves

 ## Objective
To help children realize that when they place their faith in God and follow His commandments, blessings will follow

 ## Memory Verse
He is like a tree planted by streams of water, which yields its fruit in season and whose leaf does not wither. Whatever he does prospers. **Psalm 1:3**

 ## Prayer
Dear God, how exciting it is to discover Your love in the things of nature, and to be able to share that love with others. Thank You for giving us so much. Amen.

Teach
Say, **The study of leaves shows us many things about God's creation as the leaves grow from young green sprouts to beautiful colors that gently float to the ground when the winter season arrives. They have clung to the tree throughout sunshine and rain, light breezes and strong storms. When the colored leaves have completed their cycle of life, it is great enjoyment to gather them and make arrangements to share with others. That's the way it is should be with us. If we cling to the tree which is Jesus, He will keep us through the good times and the bad and we will grow into beautiful Christians who will share our love with others.** Make the interesting fall arrangements below by turning a pumpkin into a vase to hold a bouquet of the multi-colored leaves. Make lots of tiny arrangements to take house-to-house on Halloween…leaving a bit of God's love instead of asking for treats.

You Will Need
- small pumpkins
- small can or jar
- smocks
- newspapers
- tree leaves

Before Class
Cut the "lids" off of the pumpkins. Encourage the children to wear old clothes or provide smock shirts for them to protect their clothing. For the leaves, you may provide leaves or ask the children to bring them to class. If your class meets near a wooded area you could wait until class time to take the children in search of leaves. Make sure they leave the stems intact.

What to Do
1. Spread newspapers on the work tables.
2. Show how to scoop out the loose pulp and seeds from the pumpkins. (Save the seeds and wash and dry them to add to your nature collections.)
3. Instruct the children to fill the can or jar with water and put it in the pumpkin.
4. Show how to group the leaves by their stems and insert them into the water container. If you have fall flowers available, they may be added to the leaf bouquets.

Seeking Light

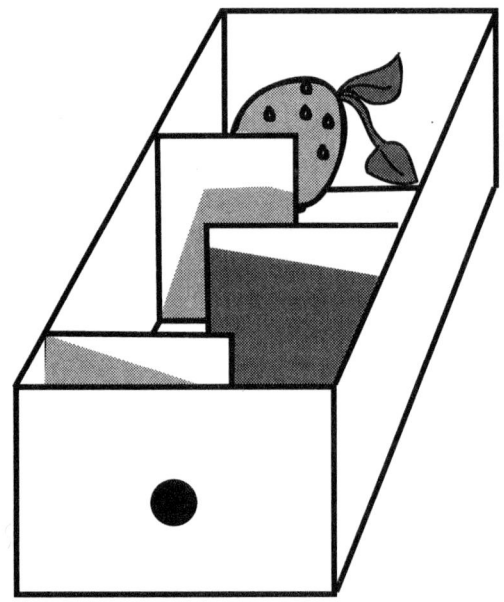

 Objective
To help children realize that just as plants need natural light to grow, we need the light of Jesus to help us grow

 Memory Verse
I have come into the world as a light, so that no one who believes in me should stay in darkness.
John 12:46

 Prayer
Dear God, thank You for sending Jesus to be the light of not only the world but of my own life. Amen.

Teach
Discuss how nothing can grow in total darkness. Say, **Our lives would be in total darkness if we didn't have the Bible and Jesus to help us get the light we need.** An interesting experiment to illustrate this concept may be conducted with a white potato as outlined below. Its sprouts will wiggle through a maze and come out into the light. You need no extra water because the potato carries its own.

You Will Need
• sprouted white potatoes
• shoe boxes
• light cardboard
• knife or scissors
• tape

Before Class
Cut a 3/4" hole at one end of a box near a corner for each child. Pre-cut pieces of cardboard for dividers as shown in the illustration.

What to Do
1. Give each child a pre-cut shoe box.
2. Following the illustration, show how to tape the dividers in the box.
3. Give each child a potato. Instruct the students to place the potato at the opposite end of the box from the hole.
4. Tell the children to place the lids back on their boxes.
5. Say, **Take your box home and point the hole in the box toward a window. In a couple of weeks the potato sprouts will poke through the hole and turn green. Open the box. Do you think they will be green inside? No, because they have not yet received the light.**